Stand and Deliver

A Practical Guide to Standup Meetings

T.D. Errol

Stand and Deliver

A Practical Guide to Standup Meetings.

T. D. Errol

Stand and Deliver: A Practical Guide To Standup Meetings
By T.D. Errol

Copyright © 2024 by T.D. Errol
All rights reserved. No part of this book may be reproduced or transmitted in any form or by any means, electronic or mechanical, including photocopying, recording, or any information storage and retrieval system, without the publisher's prior written permission, except where permitted by law.

Published by Errol Publishing

This is a work of nonfiction. Names, characters, businesses, places, events, and incidents are either the products of the author's imagination or used in a fictitious manner. Any resemblance to actual persons, living or dead, or events is coincidental.

Cover Design by Clifford Daiss
Edited by T.D. Errol

First Edition: October, 2024
ISBN: 9798342234436
Imprint: Independently published

Printed in the United States of America

Disclaimer

The information in this book is provided with the understanding that the author and

publisher are not rendering professional advice or services to the individual reader. The contents of this book are for informational purposes only and should not be used as a substitute for professional advice.

Check Out Other Great Offerings By T. D. Errol

Dedication

To Anne, whose love fills my heart beyond measure. There is nothing quite like my immense and unending love for you.

T.D.

Forward

Effective communication is more critical than ever in workplaces today. Teams are no longer confined to a single office or time zone. They span across cities, countries, and continents, making the need for efficient, effective meetings paramount. This is where the power of the standup meeting comes into play—a deceptively simple yet profoundly impactful tool that has reshaped how modern teams connect, collaborate, and conquer challenges together.

"Stand and Deliver: A Practical Guide to Standup Meetings" is your key to unlocking the true potential of these short, focused gatherings. It goes beyond just the basics, diving deep into the nuances of standup meetings for diverse teams. Whether you are part of a startup or an established organization, a remote team, or an office-based group, this guide is packed with practical advice, tailored strategies, and real-world examples to help you master the art of the standup.

This book stands out because it applies principles often overlooked in other resources. It does not just tell you *what* to do but also *how*. By exploring the importance of clear communication, accountability, and adaptability, this book provides a roadmap to streamline your team's interactions, ensuring that every standup meeting becomes a stepping stone toward greater productivity and success.

In the chapters ahead, you'll find actionable insights into customizing standups for your team, navigating common pitfalls, and fostering a culture of openness and continuous improvement. Whether you're a manager seeking to invigorate team dynamics or a team member wanting to make the most of every standup, this book offers something valuable.

So, get ready to stand up and deliver. When meetings are well-structured, concise, and purpose-driven, they transform from mere obligations into powerful catalysts for progress. "Stand and Deliver: A Practical Guide to Standup Meetings" will be your trusted companion on this journey, providing the tools and confidence you need to revolutionize your team's daily rhythm.

Let's rise to the occasion and step forward into a new era of teamwork. Your standup meetings will never be the same again.

Contents

Introduction	10
The Anatomy of a Standup Meeting	12
Setting the Stage for Success	17
Common Pitfalls and How to Avoid Them	22
Tailoring Standup Meetings for Your Team	27
Advanced Standup Techniques	31
Tools and Technology for Better Standups	35
Measuring the Effectiveness of Your Standups	39
Case Studies and Real-World Examples	42
Conclusion	47
Appendix	50

Introduction

Why Standup Meetings Matter

Standup meetings have become one of the most effective tools for fostering team communication, alignment, and agility. Often short and structured, these meetings act as a daily pulse check that can transform how teams collaborate, adapt to challenges, and drive projects forward. As more organizations embrace remote work and cross-functional collaboration, mastering the art of standup meetings has become essential.

A standup meeting is not just a quick huddle. It's a strategic ritual designed to streamline communication, promote transparency, and hold everyone accountable for their commitments. Unlike traditional meetings that can meander without purpose, standups are fast, focused, and action-oriented. They allow each participant to share progress, identify roadblocks, and plan their immediate next steps. This sense of rhythm keeps momentum alive and ensures that problems are addressed before they snowball into larger issues.

The importance of standup meetings in modern work culture lies in their ability to create a shared understanding among team members. When done correctly, they cultivate an environment where information flows freely, decision-making becomes swift, and team morale is consistently high. Teams no longer operate in silos; instead, they rally around shared goals, making the standup a unifying force.

Beyond communication, these meetings emphasize the principles of accountability and ownership. When each team member regularly provides updates, it reinforces a culture where individuals take responsibility for their roles. This openness boosts productivity and fosters a collaborative spirit where colleagues feel supported in overcoming obstacles. Standups allow for real-time problem-solving, bringing to light issues that might otherwise linger unnoticed until they become major setbacks.

The efficiency gained from standup meetings is another reason they matter so profoundly. In many organizations, long, unstructured meetings can become productivity drains. Standups flip this script by demanding brevity and clarity. Everyone knows their update needs to be concise and relevant, cultivating an environment where communication is meaningful and respectful of everyone's time. The result is a team focusing more, reducing the noise and distractions hindering progress.

This book, "Stand and Deliver! A Practical Guide to Standup Meetings," will explore these benefits in-depth. It is designed for leaders, managers, and team members who wish to master the principles of effective standups. Whether you want to enhance collaboration in a small startup or improve efficiency within a large organization, this guide will provide actionable insights to make your standups a driving force for success. We'll cover strategies for keeping meetings engaging, tailoring them to different team sizes, and navigating common pitfalls that can derail even the best intentions.

By the end of this book, you will have a toolkit filled with practical techniques to transform your standup meetings into a cornerstone of productivity and team cohesion. You'll learn how to foster an environment of trust, facilitate open communication, and build a culture where each team member is aligned with the collective goals. The journey starts here with a commitment to mastering the art of the standup, not just as a meeting format but as a vital practice that can propel your team toward greater accomplishments.

The Anatomy of a Standup Meeting

Key Elements of a Standup

At its core, the standup meeting is designed to keep teams aligned, informed, and unblocked. While these meetings may vary slightly depending on the team or project, there are fundamental components that remain consistent. Understanding these elements is crucial for executing standups that serve their purpose and add value to everyone involved.

Purpose: Updates, Blockers, Alignment

The essence of a standup meeting is to provide quick updates, identify any blockers, and align the team's efforts. Each participant briefly shares what they accomplished since the last meeting, what they are working on next, and whether there are any obstacles. This structure keeps communication clear and focused. The updates ensure that everyone is aware of progress, eliminating redundant work and keeping all members on the same page. When raised, blockers open the door for immediate support or follow-up after the meeting. This continuous cycle of sharing progress and addressing impediments ensures that no task falls through the cracks and that any issues are swiftly tackled.

Beyond updates and problem-solving, standups are critical alignment tools. They provide a daily opportunity for the team to recalibrate its direction based on the latest developments. By regularly coming together, the team builds a rhythm and momentum that helps to keep projects moving forward efficiently. Alignment extends beyond just tasks; it cultivates a shared understanding of priorities and fosters an environment of accountability.

Who Should Attend and Why

One of the most crucial aspects of standup meetings is determining who should be in the room. A standup meeting is typically designed for the core team involved in the project's day-to-day execution. This includes team members actively working on tasks, such as developers, designers, marketers, or any role specific to the team's mission. Having the right people in attendance ensures that updates are relevant and that blockers can be addressed promptly by those directly involved.

However, attendance should be carefully managed to avoid overcrowding the meeting with participants who do not have an active role. The presence of stakeholders or managers can sometimes be beneficial, especially if their input is needed to clear roadblocks or provide strategic direction. However, they should act as observers rather than active participants, allowing the core team to drive the meeting's content. The key is to strike a balance: having enough people to make informed decisions without turning the standup into a lengthy status report session. Standups become a powerful tool for fostering collaboration and enhancing team dynamics when the right individuals are present.

Frequency and Timing

The typical standup meeting is held daily, usually at the same time, to establish a routine. Daily standups create a sense of consistency and predictability, allowing the team to build a cadence. They're often scheduled in the morning, as this timing sets the tone for the day, providing an opportunity to review what was accomplished and plan for the tasks ahead. However, the optimal time may vary depending on the team's working hours, especially for remote or distributed teams. The key is to choose a time that suits the majority and stick with it, as this regularity contributes to the meeting's effectiveness.

While commonly daily, the frequency can be adjusted based on the team's specific needs. Some teams find that three times a week suffices, particularly if their work progresses slower. The length of the standup is another critical consideration. Ideally, it should be short and sweet—often no longer than 15 minutes. The brevity encourages participants to be concise, focusing only on what truly matters. If the meeting regularly runs longer, it may indicate that other topics, perhaps best discussed in separate sessions, are creeping into the standup. Keeping the meeting short but consistent helps maintain its purpose and ensures it remains a valuable, rather than burdensome, part of the team's routine.

These key elements—clear purpose, the right attendees, and appropriate frequency and timing—form the backbone of an effective standup meeting. When these elements are thoughtfully considered and implemented, the standup becomes a powerful practice for keeping the team aligned, informed, and agile.

The Classic Standup Format

The classic standup format's simplicity and structure make it so effective. At the heart of this format are three essential questions that guide the meeting and keep it focused. These questions help maintain the meeting's brevity while ensuring each participant shares valuable information. Let's explore each question and its significance.

The Three Key Questions:

1. **What did you do yesterday?**
   This question provides context and continuity. Each team member offers a snapshot of their progress by sharing their accomplishments since the last standup. This helps others understand how tasks evolve and whether the team is on track to meet its goals. Moreover, it promotes a sense of accountability. When everyone regularly updates on their completed tasks, it fosters a culture of reliability where commitments are taken seriously. This part of the meeting is not just a status update; it's a way to reflect on recent achievements and connect them to the project's broader objectives.

2. **What will you do today?**
   This is the forward-looking aspect of the standup. When participants outline their plan for the day, it sets clear intentions and provides a roadmap. It signals to the team what will be tackled next, which can spark collaboration if others have insights or assistance to offer. This question also helps identify potential overlaps or conflicts in the team's efforts, allowing for quick adjustments. By publicly stating their plan, team members commit to their tasks, which boosts accountability and provides a sense of direction for the day ahead. Sharing plans also allows others to align their work or provide help, creating a dynamic, cohesive team.

3. **Are there any blockers?**
   The blocker question is arguably the most critical component of the standup. It brings to light any obstacles that may hinder progress, offering an opportunity for the team to address issues in real-time. When blockers are openly discussed, it not only surfaces problems early but also invites the collective problem-solving power of the team. This transparency is crucial in maintaining momentum and ensuring challenges do not fester unnoticed. Identifying blockers also enables the team leader or manager to provide support where needed, whether it's by reallocating resources, adjusting priorities, or facilitating conversations with external stakeholders. Addressing obstacles as they arise prevents delays from spiraling into larger setbacks.

Why These Questions Work

These three questions are effective because they balance information sharing, planning, and problem-solving. They are straightforward yet comprehensive enough to provide a full picture of the team's progress and challenges. This format prevents the meeting from veering into unnecessary details or discussions that could be handled separately. Sticking to these focused prompts, standups remain quick, purposeful, and aligned with their primary goal: keeping the team informed, unblocked, and moving forward.

While the classic standup format is built around these three questions, it is also adaptable. Some teams may tweak the questions to fit their unique workflow or project requirements better. However, the essence remains: a brief check-in that centers on progress, planning, and problem-solving.

Setting the Stage for Success

Preparing for Your Standup

Preparation ensures that standup meetings are effective and valuable to the team's workflow. A successful standup doesn't just happen; it requires thoughtful consideration of the meeting's setup, the tools used, and the ground rules that guide its execution. This section explores how to prepare for standup meetings, whether in person or virtually, and the practices that keep them running smoothly.

Meeting Location and Setup (Physical or Virtual)
The location of your standup plays a pivotal role in setting the tone and dynamics of the meeting. For teams working in the same physical space, the ideal location is often a common area near a whiteboard, project board, or central workspace. A standing position helps keep the meeting short and encourages participants to stay focused. The physical setup should allow everyone to be in a circle or semi-circle, fostering inclusivity and open communication. If the team uses visual management tools like Kanban boards or charts, they should be visible to all participants to facilitate discussions.

In the case of virtual teams, a bit more planning is necessary to replicate the cohesion and energy of an in-person standup. The chosen virtual meeting platform, Zoom, Microsoft Teams, or another video conferencing tool, should be familiar to all participants. Camera use is encouraged, as it brings a personal element to the meeting and enables non-verbal cues crucial for effective communication. A stable internet connection and a quiet environment are essential to prevent disruptions. In both physical and virtual setups, the goal is to create a space where everyone feels seen, heard, and ready to engage.

Tools for Effective Communication (Timers, Apps, Video Conferencing)

The right tools can significantly enhance the quality and efficiency of your standup meetings. For in-person sessions, a simple timer can help keep discussions on track and ensure that everyone adheres to the meeting's time constraints. Using a visible timer, such as a phone or an hourglass, subtly reinforces the importance of brevity without cutting off important points.

In virtual settings, choosing the right video conferencing tool is paramount. Platforms like Zoom, Microsoft Teams, or Google Meet offer features like screen sharing and chat that can be beneficial during the meeting. Many of these tools also have built-in timers or can integrate with time-tracking apps to maintain the meeting's pace. Collaboration tools like Trello, Jira, or digital Kanban boards like Miro allow team members to visualize their work, share progress, and highlight blockers. These tools keep everyone on the same page, especially when the team is dispersed across different locations.

Dedicated standup meeting apps can be a game-changer for teams that prefer a more structured approach. Applications like Standuply or Geekbot provide templates and automated prompts that guide each participant through the classic standup format. These apps are particularly useful for asynchronous standups, where team members in different time zones can contribute updates at their convenience while still keeping the entire team informed.

Ground Rules: Brevity, Focus, No Problem-Solving During the Meeting

Establishing clear ground rules is essential to maintaining the integrity of the standup meeting. The most important rule is brevity. Standups are meant to be short and focused, typically lasting no longer than 15 minutes. Participants should be encouraged to share concise updates without delving into lengthy explanations to achieve this. Remind the team that the purpose of the standup is to inform, align, and surface obstacles, not to solve them on the spot.

Focus is another critical ground rule. Participants should stick to the three key questions discussed in the previous chapter: What did you do yesterday? What will you do today? Are there any blockers? Any topics requiring deeper discussion, such as problem-solving, should be noted and addressed separately after the meeting. This separation ensures the standup remains efficient and does not devolve into a full-blown problem-solving meeting. Additionally, creating a parking lot—a list of topics to revisit post-standup—can be a helpful way to acknowledge issues without disrupting the meeting flow.

By carefully preparing the meeting environment, utilizing the right tools, and setting clear ground rules, you lay the foundation for productive, inclusive, and effective standup meetings. When the team understands the purpose and format of the standup and is equipped with the right mindset and resources, these meetings become a catalyst for alignment, collaboration, and progress.

Building a Standup Culture

Creating a successful standup meeting goes beyond simply following a format; it requires building a culture that values and respects the standup's principles. A strong standup culture promotes accountability, encourages participation, and reinforces that these meetings are crucial to the team's workflow. Two key aspects of this culture are punctuality and clearly defined roles.

Encouraging Punctuality

Punctuality is the cornerstone of an effective standup culture. When team members arrive on time, it demonstrates respect for everyone's schedules and reinforces the meeting's importance. Standup meetings are intentionally brief, and starting late can throw off the entire rhythm, causing delays in other activities. Therefore, instilling a culture where punctuality is expected is vital.

Encouraging punctuality begins with clear communication. The standup's start time should be well-known, consistent, and respected by all participants. Scheduling the meeting simultaneously each day helps set a routine that becomes second nature. For those working remotely or across different time zones, being mindful of everyone's availability and choosing a time that works for the majority can make punctuality more achievable.

If lateness becomes a recurring issue, it may be helpful to establish some light-hearted but firm consequences, like requiring the latecomer to provide a quick summary of missed updates or to take on a fun team task. The goal is not to shame but to gently remind the team that punctuality matters. Over time, this expectation becomes ingrained, contributing to a disciplined and respectful standup culture.

Defining Roles (Facilitator, Note-Taker)

Defining roles within the standup meeting is another effective way to build a robust culture. While the standup format is simple, having specific roles ensures the meeting remains organized and on track. Two essential roles are the facilitator and the note-taker.

The **facilitator** is the person responsible for guiding the meeting. This role involves keeping the meeting focused, ensuring everyone sticks to the key questions, and maintaining the time limit. A good facilitator fosters an inclusive environment where participants feel comfortable sharing updates and blockers. They might prompt quieter team members to speak or politely steer the conversation back on track if it veers into problem-solving territory. Rotating the facilitator role among team members can be beneficial, as it gives everyone a chance to lead and reinforces the idea that standup meetings are a shared responsibility.

The **note-taker** documents key points during the standup. This can include a summary of each participant's updates, noted blockers, and any follow-up actions that need to be addressed outside the meeting. For virtual teams, the note-taker might update a shared document or project management tool in real-time, ensuring that the team has a record of what was discussed. While this role is optional, it can be particularly useful for larger teams or complex projects where keeping track of evolving priorities is essential. Like the facilitator role, the note-taking responsibility can rotate to distribute the workload fairly and encourage active participation.

Building a standup culture that values punctuality and clearly defined roles fosters an environment where these meetings can thrive. When everyone understands their part and is ready to engage, the standup becomes a ritual that strengthens the team's cohesion and productivity. The impact extends beyond the meeting, shaping a work culture that prizes communication, accountability, and continuous progress.

Common Pitfalls and How to Avoid Them

One of the most frequent challenges teams face with standup meetings is the risk of them running longer than intended. What should be a quick, focused check-in can easily spiral into lengthy discussions that drain energy and derail the team's schedule. Identifying the causes of overly long standups and implementing solutions can help ensure these meetings remain effective and valuable.

Causes and Consequences

Standups often become overly long due to several common causes. One frequent issue is participants delving into excessive detail during their updates. While it's natural to want to explain progress or blockers thoroughly, standup meetings are not the time for in-depth discussions. Another cause is problem-solving during the meeting. When a team member raises a blocker, the conversation can quickly shift to brainstorming solutions. While well-intentioned, this can waste valuable time and sidetrack the standup's purpose.

Another culprit is a lack of structure. Without a clear format or a facilitator to keep things on track, conversations can meander, turning the standup into a general status meeting. Additionally, inviting too many participants can lead to lengthy updates, especially if everyone needs to cover every detail of their work.

The consequences of overly long standups can be significant. They disrupt the flow of the day, delaying the start of focused work and creating frustration among team members. Over time, participants may start to dread these meetings, seeing them unproductive and time-consuming. This negative perception can erode the standup culture, reducing its effectiveness and undermining its role as a tool for team alignment and progress.

Solutions: Timeboxing, Strict Facilitation
Solutions like timeboxing and strict facilitation are essential to keep standups brief and focused. **Timeboxing** is a simple yet powerful technique. Set a firm time limit for the meeting, typically 15 minutes, and communicate this expectation to all participants. A timer or clock visible to everyone during the meeting reinforces this boundary. When participants know they have a limited window to share updates, they're more likely to be concise and stick to the key points. If the meeting consistently exceeds the time limit, revisiting the standup format or identifying specific topics that should be handled in separate discussions may be necessary.

Strict facilitation is another critical solution. The facilitator guides the meeting and ensures it adheres to its intended structure. They should gently steer conversations back on track if they start to delve into problem-solving or go off-topic. If a blocker is raised, the facilitator can acknowledge it and suggest that the discussion be continued after the standup. This practice helps keep the standup moving while ensuring that important issues are not ignored. It can also be helpful to set guidelines for each participant's update, such as limiting it to one minute, to enforce brevity further.

By identifying the causes of overly long standups and implementing solutions like timeboxing and strict facilitation, teams can maintain the efficiency and effectiveness of these meetings. A concise, focused standup respects everyone's time and reinforces its role as a quick, valuable touchpoint that drives the team forward.

Unengaged Participants

An effective standup meeting relies on active participation from every team member. However, it's common to encounter unengaged participants who appear distracted, disinterested, or hesitant to contribute. Addressing this lack of focus or participation is essential to maintaining the standup's purpose and value.

Addressing Lack of Focus or Participation

Engagement in standup meetings can stem from various causes. Some team members might feel that their updates aren't relevant or that the meeting doesn't add value to their work. Others might be overwhelmed by the pace of discussions or unsure what is expected of them. Virtual standups can exacerbate this issue, as it's easier for participants to zone out or become distracted when not physically present.

Creating an inclusive and welcoming environment where everyone feels their input is valued is crucial to tackling engagement. The first step is to remind the team of the standup's purpose: alignment, problem-solving, and shared progress. When participants understand that their contributions directly impact the team's success, they're more likely to be engaged.

Facilitators play a key role here. They can encourage quieter team members by inviting them to share their updates, using gentle prompts like, "How did your work go yesterday?" or "Do you foresee any blockers today?" This gives the less vocal participants a nudge and signals to the group that every member's input is important. However, it's essential to approach this carefully, respecting individual comfort levels and avoiding putting anyone on the spot too harshly.

Another strategy is to rotate the **facilitator role** among the team members. When individuals take turns leading the standup, they gain a new perspective on its dynamics and are likelier to stay engaged. This practice also reinforces the idea that the standup is a shared responsibility, not just a ritual led by one person.

Video can significantly improve engagement in virtual standups. When participants can see each other, it adds a personal element to the meeting and makes it easier to pick up on nonverbal cues. Collaboration tools, like shared boards or notes, where everyone can contribute in real-time, also help maintain focus and involvement.

If disengagement persists, it might be helpful to revisit the standup format with the team and ask for feedback on what's working and what could be improved. Sometimes, small tweaks—like adjusting the meeting time, refining the questions asked, or limiting the number of attendees—can make a significant difference in re-engaging participants.

By actively addressing the lack of focus or participation, you cultivate a standup culture that values every voice. Engaged participants lead to more meaningful updates, better problem-solving, and stronger team cohesion, ultimately driving the team's success.

Lack of Follow-Through

One of the main pitfalls of standup meetings is a lack of follow-through on the action items discussed. When blockers are identified, or tasks are planned but not tracked effectively, the standup loses its impact, becoming more of a routine than a driver for progress. Ensuring that action items are tracked and completed is key to making standup meetings a true catalyst for team success.

How to Ensure Action Items are Tracked and Completed

The first step to addressing this issue is establishing a clear process for capturing action items during the standup. It is essential to design a **note-taker** to document key points, including action items and their owners. This doesn't need to be overly detailed; a simple list of tasks and responsibilities will suffice. If using project management tools like Jira, Trello, or Asana, the note-taker can directly update the relevant boards during or immediately after the meeting, ensuring that action items are not forgotten.

Assigning ownership to each action item is crucial. When a team member agrees to take on a task, their name should be explicitly linked to it verbally during the standup or within the tracking tool. This clarifies who is responsible and reinforces a sense of accountability. It becomes part of the following standup's routine to revisit these action items, providing a natural checkpoint for the team. A simple, "Last standup, you mentioned tackling [specific task]; any updates?" helps keep everyone accountable while offering a moment to address any new challenges or delays.

Visual tools play a significant role in tracking follow-through. Physical or digital Kanban boards, task lists, or shared documents where tasks are marked as "In Progress," "Blocked," or "Completed" provide a visual representation of progress. These tools make it easy for everyone to see pending tasks and who is responsible. The visibility of these boards serves as a constant reminder of ongoing commitments and makes it easier to identify when things fall behind.

Consider incorporating a **brief reflection** into the standup's conclusion to encourage follow-through. The facilitator can use this moment to summarize key action items and, if appropriate, acknowledge completed tasks from the previous meeting. This simple recap reinforces the importance of following through and provides a sense of closure to the meeting.

Another strategy to ensure action items are not lost is to create a **"parking lot"** or follow-up list for topics that require deeper discussion. This list is separate from the standup and can be reviewed during a more suitable meeting, allowing it to maintain its focus while still capturing important points.

Ultimately, ensuring follow-through is about creating a rhythm of accountability. When action items are consistently tracked, revisited, and discussed in each standup, the team builds a culture where commitments are seen through to completion. This makes the standup more effective and fosters a work environment where trust and productivity thrive.

Tailoring Standup Meetings for Your Team

Customizing for Different Team Sizes

Small vs. Large Teams:
For small teams, standup meetings can be more intimate and flexible. Team members have more room to discuss details and collaborate on problem-solving during the meeting. However, maintaining structure is essential to avoid drifting into lengthy discussions. A standup for a small team often benefits from a more conversational tone, focusing on individual contributions while keeping the meeting brief and to the point.

In contrast, large teams require a more structured approach to maintain focus and efficiency. With many members present, standups can quickly become unproductive if not properly managed. A useful strategy is to limit each member's speaking time and emphasize concise updates. For particularly large teams, consider breaking the standup into smaller sub-team meetings followed by a summary for the whole group. This way, only key information is escalated, keeping the standup relevant for everyone.

Handling Remote and Hybrid Standups:
Remote and hybrid teams introduce unique challenges to standup meetings. Technology is critical for these meetings to run smoothly. Use video conferencing tools with reliable audio and video to ensure every team member can participate, regardless of location. Encourage camera use to foster a sense of presence and connection among team members, though be mindful of individual preferences and potential bandwidth issues.

Ensuring equal participation is crucial for hybrid teams, where some members are co-located and others are remote. One effective approach is to have all participants join the meeting from their own devices, even if some are physically in the same office. This creates a level playing field and prevents remote team members from feeling like outsiders. Additionally, consider using digital collaboration tools like shared boards or chat applications to document updates and track ongoing tasks, making information accessible to everyone.

Adapting to Different Methodologies

Agile, Scrum, Kanban, and Beyond:
Standup meetings can be adapted to fit various methodologies, each with its unique approach to managing work and progress. Understanding these differences helps tailor standups to support the team's goals and processes.

Agile:
In Agile environments, standups foster collaboration and align the team on goals. They serve as a daily checkpoint to identify roadblocks and ensure everyone works towards the same objectives. In this context, the standup is less about strict reporting and more about continuous improvement. The meeting typically revolves around three questions: What did you accomplish yesterday? What will you work on today? Are there any obstacles in your way? Adapting standups to an Agile framework means focusing on flexibility and using the meeting to adjust plans as needed rather than following a rigid script.

Scrum:
Scrum is a specific Agile framework that emphasizes structured, time-boxed sprints. Standups, known in Scrum as daily scrums, are vital for keeping the sprint on track. They usually last no more than 15 minutes and focus on progress toward sprint goals. Scrum standups often follow a format where each member answers the same three questions, maintaining a consistent rhythm. Adapting the standup for Scrum means

ensuring discussions are tightly scoped to sprint objectives and using the meeting to make immediate adjustments to keep the sprint moving smoothly.

Kanban:
Kanban emphasizes flow and the continuous movement of work items through various stages. Standup meetings in Kanban settings focus on the state of the workflow rather than individual contributions. The team might review the Kanban board together, discussing any bottlenecks, blocked items, or tasks that need attention. The meeting aims to maintain an efficient flow rather than simply checking off completed tasks. Adapting the standup for Kanban involves shifting the focus from individual status updates to a broader view of the work process, emphasizing work movement through the board.

Beyond Traditional Frameworks:
For teams not following a strict Agile, Scrum, or Kanban methodology, standups can be customized to suit their unique workflows. Depending on the team's goals, this might involve using the meeting for brainstorming, strategic planning, or status reporting. The key is to identify the most valuable information to share daily and how the meeting can best support the team's progress, regardless of the framework in use.

Cross-Functional Teams

How to Ensure Relevance Across Varied Roles:
Cross-functional teams bring together individuals with different expertise and responsibilities, such as developers, designers, marketers, and project managers. While this diversity is a strength, it can make standup meetings more complex. To ensure relevance and engagement across varied roles, the standup must be carefully structured to address the needs of all participants.

First, establish a common ground by focusing the meeting on shared goals and progress. Encourage team members to frame their updates in a way that highlights how their work impacts the overall project or addresses cross-team objectives. This approach prevents the meeting from becoming a series of isolated status reports and fosters collective progress. For example, rather than providing technical jargon specific to their role, team members can focus on key outcomes or challenges that other roles may need to be aware of.

Another strategy is to rotate meeting facilitation among different team roles. This practice gives everyone a sense of ownership and brings diverse perspectives to the forefront. When team members from various functions take turns leading the standup, it naturally encourages a broader view of the project's progress and needs.

Creating a flexible standup agenda that allows for brief, role-specific updates while keeping most of the meeting centered on common priorities is beneficial. For instance, the meeting can start with an overview of critical issues affecting the entire team before diving into individual updates. By setting this structure, team members can tailor their contributions to what's most relevant for the group, ensuring that the meeting remains engaging and informative for everyone involved.

Lastly, consider using visual aids like shared dashboards or boards to track progress on cross-functional tasks. These tools provide a unified view of the team's work and make it easier for members from different roles to see where their contributions fit the bigger picture. This visual element can help keep the meeting focused on the team's collective goals, ensuring that each update contributes to a cohesive understanding of the project's status.

Advanced Standup Techniques

Rotating Facilitation

Encouraging Ownership and Leadership Development:
Rotating the facilitation of standup meetings is a powerful technique for encouraging ownership and fostering leadership skills within the team. When the role of the facilitator shifts among team members, everyone takes the lead, providing a sense of responsibility and engagement. This practice helps build a culture of shared ownership where the success of the standup, and consequently the project, is seen as a collective effort.

Regarding leadership development, rotating facilitation allows individuals to practice essential skills like communication, time management, and guiding discussions. Each team member learns how to keep the meeting on track, address roadblocks, and encourage meaningful contributions from others. This experience enhances their ability to lead effective meetings and strengthens their confidence in managing other collaborative processes within the team.

To implement this rotation effectively, it's helpful to establish some basic guidelines and training for new facilitators. For example, provide a checklist or set of best practices that outlines how to prepare for the meeting, keep the conversation focused, and engage participants from different roles. Over time, as team members become more comfortable with facilitating, they can introduce their style and techniques, enriching the standup experience with diverse perspectives.

Additionally, rotating facilitation can uncover hidden leadership potential within the team. Some members who might not typically take on a leadership role may excel at guiding discussions or motivating others. This discovery can lead to greater opportunities for professional growth and a more dynamic team environment.

Encouraging everyone to step into the facilitator role makes the team more adaptable. If the usual facilitator is absent, others can seamlessly step in, ensuring that the standup continues to run smoothly. This flexibility is particularly valuable in fast-paced or dynamic project environments, where leadership needs can change rapidly.

Standup Variations

Check-ins for Non-Development Teams (e.g., Marketing, Operations):
Standup meetings aren't just for development or technical teams. They can be adapted to fit the unique needs of various departments, including marketing, operations, sales, and more. For non-development teams, standups often focus on key priorities, upcoming campaigns, or operational milestones rather than the progress of software features. The aim is to ensure alignment and identify any support needed to achieve goals.

In marketing teams, for example, a standup meeting might involve quick updates on the status of campaigns, content creation, and social media strategies. Team members can share upcoming launch dates, discuss challenges, and highlight where collaboration with other departments is necessary. For operations teams, standups might revolve around the status of key projects, inventory management, logistics issues, or customer service metrics. This variation emphasizes cross-departmental dependencies and ensures that operational tasks align with overall business objectives.

Tailoring the standup format to the team's workflow is important to keep these check-ins relevant and effective. Non-development standups can benefit from a slightly longer discussion on strategic priorities, allowing time for members to highlight how their work impacts the team's broader goals. Visual aids, like marketing calendars or operational dashboards, can also be incorporated to provide a quick overview and keep the conversation focused.

Lightning Round Standups:
Lightning round standups are an effective variation in fast-paced environments or when time is of the essence. These standups are short, sharp, and to the point, lasting no more than 5-10 minutes. Each participant provides a rapid-fire update, focusing only on what is most critical. The aim is to quickly surface any blockers or urgent items that need immediate attention.

The key to a successful lightning round standup is brevity. Team members should be encouraged to distill their updates to the essentials. This approach keeps the meeting moving and trains team members to prioritize what information they share. A simple format, such as "Yesterday, Today, Blockers," can help guide participants to deliver concise and relevant updates.

Lightning round standups work particularly well for well-coordinated teams or situations where daily progress is highly dynamic, such as during product launches, event planning, or peak operational periods. This format helps maintain momentum while minimizing the disruption to the team's workflow, making it an invaluable tool for busy teams.

Daily Syncs vs. Traditional Standups

When to Use Each Method:
Traditional standups and daily syncs serve similar purposes in keeping a team aligned and informed but differ in structure and focus. Knowing when to use each method can significantly impact team productivity and collaboration.

Traditional Standups are more structured and usually follow a set format. They often revolve around the three key questions: What did you do yesterday? What will you do today? Are there any blockers? This format works well for teams that need a consistent, disciplined approach to tracking progress, especially in development environments where tasks are interdependent. Standups are ideal when the team benefits from a predictable routine that fosters accountability and provides a daily checkpoint to identify issues early.

Standups are best suited for projects with a clear roadmap and milestones. They help keep everyone on track and focused on immediate objectives, making them highly effective in Scrum, Agile, and Kanban settings. If your team works on complex projects that require frequent plan adjustments or rely heavily on cross-functional collaboration, traditional standups offer the necessary structure to ensure alignment.

Daily Syncs, on the other hand, are more flexible and less formal. They focus on sharing information quickly and efficiently without the rigid structure of a traditional standup. Daily syncs can include status updates, quick announcements, and even brief problem-solving discussions. They are particularly useful for teams that operate in fast-paced or evolving environments, where the nature of work changes frequently, and a more dynamic communication method is needed.

Use daily syncs when the goal is to chat and maintain a high-level overview of the team's activities rather than track specific task progress. For example, in marketing, sales, or operations teams, daily syncs allow for rapid information exchange, adapting to shifting priorities, and addressing immediate needs without getting bogged down in detailed reporting. Additionally, daily syncs are beneficial for remote or hybrid teams that need to stay connected and communicate changes quickly but without the formality of a standup.

In summary, traditional standups are best used when structure, accountability, and tracking specific progress are the priorities. Daily syncs are more suitable when flexibility, rapid information exchange, and adapting to change are essential. The choice between the two depends on the team's workflow, project requirements, and the level of detail needed to keep the team moving forward effectively.

Tools and Technology for Better Standups

Popular Standup Tools

Asynchronous Standup Platforms (e.g., Slack, Trello):
As teams become increasingly distributed, asynchronous standup platforms have gained popularity. These tools allow team members to provide timely updates, accommodating different time zones and schedules. Slack and Trello are commonly used platforms that support asynchronous standups while fostering team communication and collaboration.

With **Slack,** teams can create a dedicated standup channel where each member posts their daily update, often using a predefined template. This approach provides flexibility, as team members can share their progress, plans, and blockers whenever they are ready. Slack also allows for quick follow-up discussions in threads, keeping the main standup channel focused and uncluttered. Additionally, integrations with tools like Jira or Asana can automatically pull in relevant task information, providing a more comprehensive overview.

On the other hand, Trello offers a visual way to conduct asynchronous standups. Team members can update cards on a shared board to reflect daily progress. Using columns like "Yesterday," "Today," and "Blockers," teams can quickly see the status of each task. Trello's visual nature makes it easy to track the flow of work, and its flexibility allows teams to customize the board to suit their workflow. Comments on cards enable asynchronous discussion, so team members can provide input or address issues without needing to meet in real time.

Asynchronous standup platforms are particularly useful for remote or hybrid teams where synchronizing schedules can be challenging. They provide a transparent, accessible way to keep everyone informed while allowing individuals to engage on their own time.

Virtual Whiteboards and Team Dashboards:
Virtual whiteboards and dashboards are valuable tools for enhancing standup meetings for teams that prefer a more visual approach. These platforms, such as **Miro**, **MURAL**, and **Microsoft Teams Whiteboard**, allow teams to collaborate in real-time or asynchronously, visually representing tasks, workflows, and progress.

Miro and **MURAL** provide versatile digital canvases on which teams can create standup boards, task lists, or process flows. Members can share their updates, highlight blockers, and rearrange tasks using virtual sticky notes to reflect priorities. These virtual whiteboards support interactive elements like charts, diagrams, and images, making them dynamic ways to communicate complex information. Their collaborative nature also means team members can make updates simultaneously, allowing for a more engaging and participatory standup experience.

Team dashboards, such as those in **Jira**, **Asana**, or **Notion**, centralize project data and task status in one place. During standups, teams can review these dashboards for a quick overview of progress, deadlines, and outstanding issues. Dashboards can be customized to include widgets or charts that display key metrics, helping the team focus on the most critical aspects of their work. These tools offer the flexibility of live updates and the ability to dig deeper into specific tasks or projects directly from the dashboard, making them highly efficient for standup meetings.

By incorporating these digital tools, standup meetings can become more interactive, informative, and adaptable, catering to the needs of both co-located and distributed teams.

Tracking Progress and Accountability

Integrating Task Management Software (Jira, Asana):
Task management software like **Jira** and **Asana** are powerful tools for tracking progress and maintaining accountability during standup meetings. By integrating these platforms into your standup routine, teams can have a centralized source of truth for all tasks, ensuring that updates are based on real-time data and everyone is aligned on priorities.

Jira is particularly popular among development teams, as it is designed to manage software projects with complex workflows. During standups, teams can use Jira's dashboard to review ongoing tasks, assess progress on user stories, and quickly identify blockers. Each task or issue in Jira contains detailed information, such as status, priority, assigned team members, and relevant documentation. This level of detail allows for more meaningful discussions during standups, as team members can reference the exact status of their work and provide precise updates.

Jira also supports integration with tools like Slack, Confluence, and GitHub, creating a seamless ecosystem for tracking work across various development lifecycle stages. By linking standup updates directly to Jira issues, teams maintain transparency and accountability, ensuring that progress is documented and any changes are easily traceable.

Asana is another versatile tool that suits various teams, from marketing to operations. It provides an intuitive interface for creating tasks, setting deadlines, assigning responsibilities, and tracking progress. During standups, teams can pull up their Asana project board to discuss completed tasks, upcoming priorities, and any roadblocks. The platform's customizable views—such as lists, boards, and calendars—make it easy to tailor the discussion to the team's workflow.

Asana's **task comments** and **project notes** features enable asynchronous communication, allowing team members to provide updates or request help directly within the task. This integration fosters accountability, as everyone's contributions are visible and accessible.

Moreover, Asana's reporting features can generate progress charts and workload balances, providing valuable insights for the team to discuss during standups.

Integrating tools like Jira and Asana into standup meetings streamlines progress tracking and reinforces accountability. By using these platforms, teams can ensure that standup discussions are grounded in up-to-date information, helping keep projects on track and making addressing any issues as they arise easier.

Measuring the Effectiveness of Your Standups

How to Measure Success

Productivity Metrics, Team Satisfaction, Reduced Meeting Times:
Establishing clear success criteria is crucial for assessing the effectiveness of standup meetings. While the primary goal of a standup is to keep the team aligned and address any roadblocks, its effectiveness can be measured through various metrics and feedback mechanisms.

Productivity Metrics:
One way to gauge the success of standups is by tracking productivity metrics. Look for changes in the completion rate of tasks, user stories, or project milestones before and after implementing or adjusting standups. For example, suppose the team starts completing tasks more quickly and efficiently. In that case, the standup meetings effectively identify bottlenecks and keep everyone focused on high-priority items.

Additionally, tracking the average time it takes to resolve blockers reported during standups can provide insights into the meeting's impact. If blockers are being addressed more swiftly, it suggests that the standups serve their purpose in facilitating quick problem-solving and fostering a collaborative environment.

Team Satisfaction:
Another key measure of success is the team's overall sentiment toward the standup meetings. If team members find standups valuable, they are more likely to participate and engage in meaningful discussions actively. Regular feedback surveys can be an effective way to gauge team satisfaction. Simple questions like "Do you find the daily standup

helpful?" or "Do the standups improve your understanding of the team's progress?" can reveal whether the meetings meet the team's needs.

Observing team dynamics during standups also provides valuable qualitative feedback. The standup fosters a positive and productive team culture if team members openly discuss their progress, offer help, and proactively address issues. Conversely, if the standup feels like a mere formality, with little engagement or interaction, it may signal the need for adjustments in format or focus.

Reduced Meeting Times:
A successful standup should be short and focused, ideally lasting no more than 15 minutes. Monitoring the duration of standup meetings can help measure their efficiency. If the meetings run consistently longer than intended, it might indicate that discussions are veering off track or that the agenda is too broad. Implementing changes like tightening the format or using timeboxing for individual updates can help streamline the process.

A reduction in the overall time spent in meetings throughout the week can also reflect the effectiveness of standups. When standups provide the necessary information and alignment, teams may require fewer additional meetings, freeing up more time for productive work.

By evaluating these aspects—productivity metrics, team satisfaction, and meeting times—you can better understand how well your standups are working and identify areas for continuous improvement.

Continuous Improvement

Gathering Feedback and Evolving the Process:
The effectiveness of standup meetings can be significantly enhanced through a continuous improvement mindset. Regular feedback from the team is crucial for evolving the standup process to meet changing needs and challenges. This feedback can be collected in various ways, such as informal check-ins, surveys, or dedicated feedback sessions. Encourage team members to share their thoughts on the meeting's structure,

content, and duration. Simple questions like "What aspects of the standup are most helpful?" and "What changes would make the standup more effective?" can spark valuable insights.

The team can make incremental adjustments to improve the standup based on the feedback. This might involve altering the format, changing the meeting time to better suit everyone's schedules, or adjusting the focus to address different aspects of the workflow. The key is to keep the process flexible and responsive, ensuring that standups continue to serve the team's evolving needs. By fostering a culture of openness and experimentation, teams can develop a standup routine that consistently adds value.

Retrospectives on Standup Effectiveness:
Just as retrospectives are used to reflect on a team's work process, conducting periodic retrospectives, specifically on the standup meetings, can provide a focused opportunity to evaluate their impact. During these retrospectives, the team can discuss what has worked well in the standups and identify areas for improvement. This review helps to uncover patterns—such as recurring blockers, lengthy discussions, or lack of engagement—that may signal the need for changes.

In a standup retrospective, consider using prompts like "What aspects of our standup meetings are helping us stay on track?" or "What could we change to make our standups more efficient?" This structured reflection allows the team to step back and assess how well the standups align with their goals, promoting a mindset of continuous optimization.

These retrospectives help refine the standup process and reinforce the principle that standups are a collaborative effort where everyone's input is valued. By regularly revisiting and fine-tuning the standup format, teams ensure that the meetings remain relevant, engaging, and effective in driving productivity and teamwork.

Case Studies and Real-World Examples

Examples from Different Industries

Tech Startups:
In tech startups, teams often work in fast-paced and dynamic environments; standup meetings are vital for maintaining alignment and momentum. For example, a software development startup might conduct daily standups with a clear focus on progress and blockers related to sprint goals. The team gathers in a casual, open space to review their updates, keeping discussions brief and to the point. Due to the startup's small size, everyone gets a chance to speak, which fosters a sense of collective ownership over the product's development. The team also uses digital tools like Jira and Slack to facilitate asynchronous updates, making it easy to keep track of tasks and issues outside the meeting.

In this context, standup becomes a cornerstone of the agile development process, enabling rapid adjustments to the work plan. The startup's ability to adapt quickly is reflected in its standup style, which is flexible, concise, and heavily focused on removing obstacles that could slow down its tight timelines.

Marketing Teams:
Marketing teams often manage multiple campaigns, deadlines, and creative projects. Therefore, they benefit from standups that emphasize cross-functional collaboration. For example, a marketing team at a mid-sized company might hold a daily check-in to sync on ongoing campaigns, content creation, and promotional strategies. Unlike development-focused standups, these meetings might include discussions about market trends, customer feedback, and creative ideas.

For example, in a marketing agency, the standup may start with an overview of current campaigns, followed by updates from team members working on different aspects such as social media, content production, and analytics. The team might use a Trello board to visualize their tasks and project stages, helping everyone see the workflow and identify bottlenecks. By focusing on strategic and operational elements, marketing standups ensure that creative efforts align with broader business goals.

Product Development:
In product development environments, standups are crucial for coordinating cross-functional teams, including designers, engineers, and product managers. A consumer electronics company, for instance, might use standups to review the status of product design, testing, and manufacturing. The team meets daily to discuss progress, address issues with prototypes, and align on upcoming deadlines.

During these standups, the team might use a Kanban board to visualize the product's development stages. This allows members to quickly spot which phase a particular component is in and where bottlenecks might occur. The standup serves as a status update and an opportunity for immediate problem-solving, with team members from different specialties offering input to resolve technical or design challenges. This cross-functional focus helps maintain a steady product development pace while ensuring every team member has visibility into the entire product lifecycle.

Remote Work Environments:
Standup meetings are especially important for remote teams to foster communication and cohesion. A fully remote software development company might conduct daily standups via video conferencing tools like Zoom or Microsoft Teams. To accommodate different time zones, they often employ asynchronous standup platforms, where team members post their updates in a shared Slack channel at a time that suits them.

In this setting, the standup becomes more than just a progress update—it's a touchpoint that helps maintain a sense of connection among remote workers. Visual tools like shared whiteboards or digital Kanban boards are used during meetings to keep everyone engaged and provide a visual context for discussions. The focus on flexibility and inclusion ensures that all team members, regardless of location, can contribute effectively to the standup, maintaining the team's overall alignment and productivity.

These examples illustrate how standups can be tailored to fit the specific needs of different industries and team structures. Standups are a versatile tool for enhancing communication, accountability, and workflow in a fast-paced tech startup, a creative marketing team, product development, or a fully remote work environment.

Lessons Learned from Successes and Failures

Depending on how they are conducted, standup meetings can either be a catalyst for team productivity or a drain on time and energy. Learning from successful and failed implementations can help refine the process and maximize the benefits of standup meetings.

Successes:
One of the key lessons from successful standups is the importance of maintaining structure while allowing flexibility. For example, a tech startup that adopted standups early on found that having a consistent format—asking the three fundamental questions about yesterday's work, today's plans, and blockers—kept meetings focused and efficient. However, they also allowed some flexibility, allowing team members to bring up urgent issues that didn't fit neatly into the usual format. This balance of structure and adaptability helped the team stay aligned while addressing emerging problems in real time.

Another lesson from success is the power of visual aids. Teams that use tools like Kanban boards, digital dashboards, or whiteboards during their standups report higher engagement and a clearer understanding of work progress. By incorporating visual elements, standups become more dynamic and informative, making tracking task status easier and identifying areas requiring attention.

Lastly, successful teams emphasize the value of brevity. A marketing team that regularly completes standups in under 10 minutes attributes its success to staying focused on key updates and avoiding deep dives into problem-solving during the meeting. By saving detailed discussions for separate sessions, they keep the standup effective and energizing, leaving team members with a clear direction for the day.

Failures:
Conversely, some teams have learned from their mistakes when standups didn't go as planned. A common pitfall is allowing standups to devolve into long, unfocused discussions. A product development team once experienced this issue when team members began using the meeting to solve complex problems. As a result, their standups stretched to 30 minutes or more, leaving participants feeling drained and frustrated. The lesson was the need to enforce timeboxing and redirect deep discussions to separate, dedicated problem-solving sessions.

Another failure involves a lack of engagement, particularly in remote teams. A fully remote company initially struggled with its standups because they were conducted asynchronously through a chat platform without visual aids or video interactions. Over time, team members became less engaged, providing minimal updates or skipping the process altogether. The team learned that simply posting text updates was insufficient to maintain a sense of connection. They improved their standups by incorporating video calls at least once weekly and using shared dashboards for visual context, significantly boosting participation and team morale.

Finally, neglecting retrospectives on standup effectiveness can lead to stagnation. Some teams that have failed to review and adjust their standup process periodically have found that the meetings become repetitive and lose their value over time. Learning from this, successful teams regularly reflect on their standup format, adjusting based on feedback and changing needs to keep the meetings fresh, relevant, and productive.

In both successes and failures, the overarching lesson is that the effectiveness of standups hinges on continuous evaluation and adaptation. By learning from what works and what doesn't, teams can refine their standup process to support communication, accountability, and progress better.

Conclusion

The Future of Standup Meetings

Adapting Standups to Changing Work Environments:
The nature of work has been rapidly evolving, and standup meetings are no exception. The increasing prevalence of remote work, hybrid teams, and global collaboration has reshaped how we communicate and coordinate. As organizations navigate these shifts, standup meetings must adapt to remain a valuable practice.

One significant change is the move towards more **asynchronous communication**. With team members spread across different time zones, daily standups in a traditional, synchronous format may no longer be practical. To address this, teams increasingly use asynchronous platforms that allow participants to provide updates at their convenience. This flexibility accommodates diverse schedules and allows for deeper, more thoughtful contributions. Tools like Slack, Trello, and dedicated standup applications have been instrumental in supporting this shift, and their continued development will further enhance asynchronous standups. For example, future iterations of these tools include features like automated task prioritization, AI-generated summaries of key points, and even sentiment analysis to gauge team morale over time.

Virtual reality (VR) and augmented reality (AR) are also on the horizon as potential game-changers for standup meetings. Imagine a future where remote team members can join a virtual office space, interact with a shared Kanban board, and engage in real-time discussions as if they were physically present. These immersive technologies could bridge the gap between remote and in-person communication, offering a richer, more engaging standup experience.

Although still in its early stages, VR and AR standups may soon become a practical reality for forward-thinking organizations.

Maintaining Relevance as Teams Evolve:
As teams grow, take on new projects, or shift their strategies, the standup meeting must evolve to maintain its relevance. This adaptability is crucial for keeping the standup aligned with the team's goals and dynamics. For example, a small, tightly-knit startup might initially find daily, all-hands standups effective. However, as the company scales, a single standup for the entire team might become unwieldy, necessitating the introduction of sub-team standups, rotating facilitators, or lightning rounds to keep the meeting concise and focused.

Retrospectives play a vital role in this ongoing evolution. By regularly reflecting on the standup's format, content, and outcomes, teams can identify what's working, what's not, and what might need to change. This practice ensures that the standup remains a living, adaptive process rather than a static ritual. Moreover, encouraging team members to take turns facilitating standups fosters a sense of ownership and inclusivity, allowing for diverse perspectives on how the meeting can best serve the team's needs.

It's also important to consider the **team's cultural values and goals to keep the standup relevant**. For some teams, a standup might evolve to focus more on strategic alignment, where discussions center around key initiatives and long-term objectives rather than day-to-day tasks. In other cases, the emphasis might shift towards cross-functional collaboration, using the standup as a platform to identify opportunities for synergy across different roles and departments. The flexibility to adapt the standup's focus ensures it continues to deliver value, regardless of how the team's priorities or structure change over time.

Ultimately, the future of standup meetings will likely be characterized by their ability to adapt seamlessly to the changing work landscape. Whether embracing new technologies, shifting to asynchronous formats, or refining their focus to suit evolving team dynamics, standups will remain a cornerstone of effective communication and coordination. The key to their lasting success lies in their willingness to experiment, listen to team feedback, and continuously improve. As long as teams are open to evolving their standup process, this time-tested practice will continue to empower collaboration, foster accountability, and drive productivity in an ever-changing work environment.

Standup meetings are about keeping everyone on the same page and creating a shared rhythm for the team. This rhythm, whether in person, virtual, synchronous, or asynchronous, helps teams move forward, navigate challenges, and celebrate successes. As you move forward with your standup practices, remember that the best meetings evolve with your team, providing the structure and support needed to achieve great things—today, tomorrow, and the years to come.

Appendix

Sample Standup Meeting Agenda

A well-structured standup meeting agenda serves as a guide to keep the meeting focused, efficient, and productive. While each team may adapt the agenda to their needs, a typical standup follows a concise and structured flow. Here's an example of a sample agenda that teams can use as a starting point:

1. **Start with a Quick Greeting (1 minute):**
   Begin the meeting with a brief greeting to set a positive tone. A simple "Good morning, everyone!" helps create a sense of connection, especially for remote or hybrid teams. If time permits, a quick team check-in, like a "How's everyone feeling today?" can foster a collaborative atmosphere without sidetracking the meeting.

2. **Review the Meeting Format (1 minute):**
   It's helpful to quickly state the meeting's structure for newer teams or those experimenting with different formats. For example, "Today, we'll share updates on yesterday's work, today's focus, and any blockers." This brief reminder sets expectations and ensures everyone is on the same page.

3. **Team Member Updates (8–10 minutes):**
   - ✓ **Yesterday:** Each team member shared their accomplishments since the last standup. The focus should be on completed tasks, progress, and notable achievements.
   - ✓ **Today:** Next, team members state their primary focus for the current day. This helps the team understand each

other's priorities and identify potential collaboration opportunities.
- ✓ **Blockers:** Finally, each person highlights any obstacles they are facing. Blockers should be addressed briefly, with deeper discussions or problem-solving reserved after the standup. This ensures the meeting stays on track and does not become lengthy troubleshooting sessions.

To keep things moving, timebox each person's update to 1 minute or less, depending on the team size. If discussions veer into more complex problem-solving territory, the facilitator can gently guide participants to wrap up.

4. **Review Key Metrics or Board (2–3 minutes):**
   If the team uses a Kanban board, task management software, or any visual tracking tool, take a minute to review it together. Highlight any areas of concern, such as tasks that have been in progress for too long or items approaching their deadlines. This brief review helps maintain transparency and focus on the team's workflow.

5. **Quick Announcements or Reminders (1 minute):**
   Reserve a moment at the end of the standup for any quick announcements, upcoming events, or reminders. This could include anything from noting a planned team outing to reminding everyone of an upcoming project milestone.

6. **Wrap-Up and Follow-Up (1 minute):**
   Close the meeting by summarizing any key takeaways or action items. If some blockers or issues require deeper discussion, the facilitator can designate a follow-up session for those involved. This wrap-up reinforces the next steps and ensures that the standup ends on a clear and actionable note.

Total Time: 15 minutes or less

This sample agenda provides a balanced structure, allowing team members to give updates, identify obstacles, and briefly review progress while keeping the meeting short and focused. Teams can modify this agenda to fit their unique workflow, adjust the timing, add sections, or incorporate elements that suit their collaboration style. The key is maintaining a consistent rhythm and supporting the team's productivity and communication.

Checklist for Effective Standup Meetings

A checklist is a handy tool for ensuring that standup meetings are efficient, focused, and beneficial for the team. This guide can help you prepare for, facilitate, and review your standup meetings to maximize their effectiveness.

1. Preparation:
Set a Consistent Time: Have you scheduled the standup at the same time each day to create a routine that everyone can plan around?

[ ] **Select an Appropriate Location or Platform:** Is the meeting space accessible to all team members, whether physical or virtual? Have you tested the technology (e.g., video conferencing tools) to ensure a smooth experience for remote or hybrid participants?

[ ] **Update Visual Aids:** Is the task board, Kanban board, or digital dashboard updated with the latest task statuses and ready for review during the meeting?

[ ] **Send a Reminder:** Have you sent out a reminder to participants, including the agenda or any specific focus points for the day?

2. During the Standup:
[ ] **Start on Time:** Did you start the meeting promptly, respecting

everyone's schedule, even if some participants were absent?
[ ] **Set a Positive Tone:** Did you greet the team and, if possible, do a quick check-in to foster engagement and a collaborative atmosphere?
[ ] **Outline the Meeting Format:** Have you clearly stated the structure of the meeting, especially if new team members are present or if changes to the format are introduced?
[ ] **Facilitate Concise Updates:** Are team members providing brief updates on what they accomplished yesterday, what they plan to do today, and any blockers they face?
[ ] **Stay on Track:** Are you guiding the conversation to prevent deep dives into problem-solving or off-topic discussions and ensure that updates remain short and relevant?
[ ] **Highlight and Note Blockers:** Have you captured any blockers mentioned for follow-up discussions after the standup to avoid sidetracking the meeting?
[ ] **Review Visual Aids:** Did you take a moment to review the task board, dashboard, or any key metrics with the team to provide a clear overview of progress and upcoming priorities?
[ ] **Share Quick Announcements:** Did you allow time for brief announcements, updates, or reminders that impact the team's work?
[ ] **End on Time:** Are you keeping the standup within the 15-minute limit, ensuring it remains a quick and efficient part of the team's daily routine?

3. Post-Meeting Follow-Up:

[ ] **Document Key Takeaways:** Have you recorded any critical information, such as action items, identified blockers, or key decisions, for reference and accountability?
[ ] **Schedule Additional Discussions:** Have you arranged follow-up meetings for issues or blockers requiring more in-depth problem-solving outside the standup?
[ ] **Collect Team Feedback:** Are you periodically gathering feedback from the team on how the standup meetings can be improved to serve

everyone's needs better?

[ ] Review Standup Effectiveness: Are you regularly assessing the format, duration, and focus of the standup meetings to ensure they remain relevant and valuable as the team and its projects evolve?

This checklist can be adapted to suit your team's specific needs and workflows. Reviewing it regularly and incorporating these steps into your standup routine will help create meetings that are efficient, engaging, and aligned with your team's goals.

Additional Reading

To deepen your understanding of standup meetings and enhance your team's collaboration and productivity, here is a list of recommended books, articles, and resources:

1. **Books on Agile, Scrum, and Kanban:**

   "Scrum: The Art of Doing Twice the Work in Half the Time" by Jeff Sutherland. This book provides insights into Scrum methodologies, including practical tips for running effective standup meetings within the Scrum framework.

   "Kanban: Successful Evolutionary Change for Your Technology Business" by David J. Anderson. For teams exploring Kanban principles, this book offers valuable techniques for managing workflow and optimizing standups.

   "Agile Estimating and Planning" by Mike Cohn is a must-read for understanding Agile practices. It also includes valuable strategies for organizing and conducting standups that align with broader project goals.

2. **Books on Team Collaboration and Communication:**

   "Radical Candor: Be a Kick-Ass Boss Without Losing Your Humanity" by Kim Scott. This book delves into fostering open team communication, crucial for successful standups.

   "Crucial Conversations: Tools for Talking When Stakes Are High" by Kerry Patterson, Joseph Grenny, Ron McMillan, and Al Switzler. Understanding how to navigate difficult conversations and maintain focus can enhance the effectiveness of your standup meetings.

3. **Articles and Blog Posts:**

   Atlassian's Agile Coach: A comprehensive resource on agile practices, including articles on conducting standups, facilitating retrospectives, and managing team dynamics. Check out their website: www.atlassian.com/agile.

   Mountain Goat Software Blog: Mike Cohn's blog offers practical advice on agile methodologies, including tips for improving standup meetings and other agile ceremonies. Visit: www.mountaingoatsoftware.com.

4. **Online Courses and Webinars:**

   Agile and Scrum Courses on Coursera: Websites like Coursera offer various courses on Agile, Scrum, and Kanban, providing strategies to run effective standups. Look for courses like *"Agile Development Specialization"* to expand your skills.

   Pluralsight's Agile Series: Pluralsight provides a range of courses focused on agile practices, including specific modules on team collaboration and standup meetings.

5. **Additional Resources:**

   Scrum.org: A valuable resource for learning about Scrum practices, offering guides, articles, and videos that cover daily standups and other key elements of Scrum. Visit: www.scrum.org.

LeanKit Blog: For Kanban teams, LeanKit's blog offers insights into Kanban boards, workflow management, and running daily standups tailored for Kanban teams. Visit www.planview.com/resources/blog.

Thank you for choosing to read this book. If you enjoyed it or found it valuable, I would be deeply grateful if you would take a few moments to leave a review. Your feedback helps me grow as a writer and guides other readers in discovering content that speaks to them.

No matter the length, every review makes a difference, and I would love to hear your thoughts on how this book impacted you.

Again, Thank you for your time and support—it truly means the world to me.

Warm regards,

T.D. Errol